White Flash / Black Rain

White Flash / Black Rain

Women of Japan
Relive the Bomb

edited and translated by

Lequita Vance - Watkins

and

Aratani Mariko

MILKWEED
EDITIONS

Published 1995 by Milkweed Editions
Printed in the United States of America
Book design by Will Powers. The text of this book is set in Galliard.
95 96 97 98 99   5 4 3 2 1
First Edition

Milkweed Editions is a not-for-profit publisher. We gratefully acknowledge support from Target Stores, Dayton's, and Mervyn's by the Dayton Hudson Foundation; Ecolab Foundation; General Mills Foundation; Honeywell Foundation; Jerome Foundation; John S. and James L. Knight Foundation; The McKnight Foundation; Andrew W. Mellon Foundation; Minnesota State Arts Board through an appropriation by the Minnesota State Legislature; Challenge and Literature Programs of the National Endowment for the Arts; I. A. O'Shaughnessy Foundation; Piper Jaffray Companies, Inc.; John and Beverly Rollwagen Fund of the Minneapolis Foundation; The St. Paul Companies, Inc.; Star Tribune/Cowles Media Foundation; Surdna Foundation; James R. Thorpe Foundation; Lila Wallace-Reader's Digest Literary Publishers Marketing Development Program, funded through a grant to the Council of Literary Magazines and Presses; and generous individuals.

Library of Congress Cataloging-in-Publication Data

White flash, black rain / edited and translated by Lequita Vance-Watkins
    and Aratani Mariko—1st ed.
        p.   cm.
     ISBN 1-57131-402-4 (alk. paper)
     1. Hiroshima-shi (Japan)—History—Bombardment, 1945—Personal narratives.
  2. Nagasaki-shi (Japan)—History—Bombardment, 1945—Personal narratives.
  3. Atomic bomb victims—Japan—Biography.   4. Women—Japan—Biography.
  5. Hiroshima-shi (Japan)—History—Bombardment, 1945—Poetry.   6. Nagasaki-shi (Japan)—History—Bombardment, 1945—Poetry.   I. Vance-Watkins, Lequita.
  II. Aratani, Mariko.
  D767.25.H6W45   1995
  940.54'26—dc20   95-7560
                                                                          CIP

This book is printed on acid-free paper.

for
my Alexandra, her mother, Teresa,
and her uncles Christopher and John
L. V.-W.

for
Noé, in hope that no children will again
experience nuclear horror
A. M.

Acknowledgments

We would like to thank Sandra Alcosser, Tom Anderson, Bobbie Bristol, Emilie Buchwald, Tamara Burnham, Ginger Chih, Jane Hirshfield, Damon Holmes, James Mandiberg, Sherod Santos, Carol Staudacher, and Belle Yang for their support and understanding of the importance of bringing these women's voices to an English-speaking audience.

There are two people to whom we would like to give special thanks. We are grateful to Hannerl Liebmann not just for her ongoing work as typist and proofreader but for her perpetual faith and labor invested in this project from its very beginning. To Elisabeth Marshall we are most appreciative for her many long hours dedicated to proofing the manuscript for this book.

White Flash / Black Rain

Introduction

There are events that change our lives. There are events that change the lives of our community and our country, and there are events that change the world. But even those most terrifying and far-reaching are confined to a given period, to one time frame. It seems almost impossible, or at least once it seemed impossible, that any one thing could destroy forever not just our human world but all that lives on this planet.

Before August 6, 1945, such an idea was confined to the realm of science fiction. But since that Monday it has been clear that nuclear warfare has the very real and immediate capability to end the life of every living creature and substance on Earth. The signing of an unconditional surrender by the Japanese that concluded World War II did not end, but was the birthdate of, the terror of what a continuation of atomic warfare would mean.

Nuclear destruction has moved from the realm of science fiction to being an entrenched concern of each individual and of every political and scientific society. In literature, too, poets and writers have added their voices and art in protest against the use of nuclear weapons.

The women whose words speak to us in this book are voicing their desire for peace—an ongoing peace that will allow planetary life to continue without the moment-to-moment anxiety that all life could be ended, and ended forever.

These voices tell us that nuclear consequences did not end with World War II but continued in the bodies and the souls of victim and victor, the liberated, and the vanquished. This is a book of peace, but it is also a book of shared responsibility for what goes into the making of war.

Here are women telling of the disastrous path Japan was following with its policy of conquest and Emperorism in Korea and China. There are poems and stories about the treatment of "comfort women" brought to Japan for the use of Japanese soldiers and of the failure of the Japanese to bury the corpses of foreign victims of the bombing. Those events are as much the disasters of war as the immediate deaths during a bombing. In singing out the full range of shared responsibility, it is clear that each side has its own part in the chorus of war.

Our debt of gratitude to the women's voices in this collection and to all that they represent is immense. Because the possibility for nuclear warfare exists, there is always, no matter how minor the conflict, the fear and threat that any war could lead to another nuclear holocaust. Our united effort must be to ensure that it will not occur ever again. We have it in our power to demand that never again will a white flash flash or a black rain rain.

L. V.-W.

White Flash / Black Rain

haiku

eyes closed
I pick up pieces of
sunburned bones

Igasaki Shizuko

as if they were rafts
under the flaming sky
bodies flow

Ito Hiroe

fireworks reflections
at the bottom of the river
bones must be burning

Utsumi Kanko

tanka

Shoda Shinoe

Pulled
from a water tank,
the bodies of a mother and child,
their hands
inseparably clasped.

It is not coal
heaped high
on that passing truck.
It is corpses piled
high and black.

The Sky

Horiba Kiyoko

I
I want you all to know how blue the sky was
the sky toward which the millions of rain-struck and
sunburned eyes were turned

How blue the sky was
the sky
silently embracing
moans of the inflamed earth
a hell more cruel than hell
instantly imprinted for eternity on the retinas of
dead embryos

How blue the sky was
after the white parachute clouds
flew away far beyond the mountain range
their poison mushrooms floating away
on our Acheron

II
August 6, 1945
The day that stains humankind
that day the blue sky
bloomed splendid crimson and purple
a mandala of old folk tales
that swirling and roaring rose of damnation

Between mountains a narrow delta fills with the debris of
incinerated bodies . . .

A hand grasps stone in pain
crumbles, remains on stone
clothes burn away on corpses with
skin no longer skin
on others flesh gathers around wrists
like beautiful orange-colored gloves

and intestines red and purple hang
outside bodies
babies starving and bloody and
heads smashed with stones
parade, ghost monsters
marching to a place without destruction
to a world of green and of life
marching as long as their breath lasts

III
The Second Day
Pus runs blue-yellow

The Third Day
Maggots fall off living bodies

IV
Day after day
behind the butterfly of death's wings
corpses increase, laid like eggs one on another

Human grease
shines in the night
in the city of ruins

Daylight and along the hollows of riverbank sand
ashes of the unknown pile up

burned again, the burned alive
become pale blue vapor and bloody smell
giving off an invisible plea
to survivors' nostrils

Day after day
smoke rises thinly
like a grove
like vain prayers
along the river Ota
each rivulet of smoke sways and melts into
the cold, clear sky

How blue that sky was
the sky
nurtured all summer by
the smoke of corpses

V

This afternoon
in a suburban hospital a woman
wraps her big belly with
a borrowed *yukata*
its thin sash hangs limp on the straw mat

*A crowd of the severly injured is taken away. Stench and moans
saturate the walls and straw mats. The footprints and signs of death
are everywhere. . . .*

And a woman alone
looks motionlessly
at the sky

*A nurse whispers, "She has a wound in her belly and has lost all her
water." "She and the baby will not live," the doctor says.*

Blue-black the woman's face
already enters the circle of death
her eyes staring
at the blue sky

What does she see
over the ruins and corpses, over the ashes and rubble
in this cobalt blue sky?

yukata — lightweight summer kimono

A Child Remembers

Tanaka Kiyoko

This account was recalled by Tanaka Kiyoko when she was in the ninth grade, six years after she had experienced the bombing on August 6, 1945.

I was in the third grade the day the unforgettable happened: the atomic bomb was dropped on Hiroshima. Even now I tremble when I think of that day.

I had not been evacuated like some of the children. I could stay at home with my parents and study in my class even during the war. But that day I had gone with a friend to visit my neighbor. We were playing there when the Flash came, and I was suddenly buried under the collapsed house. I had no idea what would happen next; then I saw a small gap in the rubble. I crawled over to it, pushed aside a board, and managed to get outside. At first I thought only the house I was in had been burned by fire. But then I saw that all the other houses were burning or had been destroyed.

Frightened, I began to cry but knew it would not help, so instead I started home to find my family.

When I got to my house, I found my mother in the street trying to move all our belongings outside. Her one-year-old baby was lying in shock on a nearby pile of luggage.

My mother was happy and relieved to see me and said that we must flee quickly or we would be burned alive. She put the baby on her back, took up what she could carry, and we left our home to try to find safety.

As we left, there was a man near us who could see nothing because there was a large piece of wood sticking out of one of his eyes. He was moving crazily about, not knowing what to do or where to go.

We ran along in the same direction that everyone else was running, but no one knew where they were going. We found ourselves headed toward Hiji-yama, and along the way saw many people jumping into water tanks and ponds trying to escape the pain of their burning. Some were squatting along the road begging for water to be poured on them or to be given a drink. Others were drinking muddy water from the side of the road.

Just as we were about to reach Hiji-yama, we saw a giant tree burning from its middle. As we got to the top of the mountain, we looked down and saw that the entire area was one great ocean of fire. Around us, burned and injured people covered the entire mountaintop, and they filled the air with their cries and moaning.

We climbed down the other side of the mountain and walked toward Danbara. Although it was not burning, most of its houses had been destroyed by the blast and were only shells.

People were fleeing all around us. Some of them were barefoot; they stopped at houses where wooden clogs stood outside, put them on, and ran away as fast as they could.

We continued walking and after some time heard a man shouting through a megaphone. He was telling the injured to go to Ninoshima Island. My mother decided that we, too, should go there, so we boarded a boat with them and started across the river.

On the boat was a girl just about my own age. Her whole body was burned and bleeding. She called and called for her mother, but there was no answer. Suddenly, because she could no longer see, she asked my mother if there was a child with her. My mother told her that the baby and I were there.

"Then, Auntie, give this to your little girl," she said and handed the lunch box she was still clutching to my mother. As soon as I saw it, I realized it must be the lunch her mother had packed for her before she left for school that morning.

"Aren't you going to eat it yourself?" my mother asked gently.

8

"I can't," she said. "I can no longer keep anything in my stomach, so let your daughter eat it."

Silently, both Mother and I ate the lunch.

We traveled for some time down the river and came to the ocean. At that point the girl spoke once more, "I will tell you my name so if you see my mother you can tell her where I am." Those were her last words, for the next moment she died.

Her death made us so sad that both my mother and I cried and cried for a long time.

At last we got to Ninoshima Island, where there was set up a camp for victims of the attack. It was packed with the burned and injured. Among them, running wild and frantic, were those driven mad by the terror of the day. Many of those suffering died that day, and others afterward.

Today I know how much happier I would be if they had not had to die . . . and if the little girl who gave us her lunch had lived and was here today with her mother.

The Second Room
(Chonum yogie issumnida, *I am here*)

Ishikawa Itsuko

The title refers to a place called Chidorigahuchi Senbotsusha
Boen, *in Tokyo, where the bones of the bombing victims were kept.
The basement there was divided into six rooms, and this second room
is where Ishikawa contemplated the fate of Korean women brought to
Japan for the use of Japanese soldiers. Though there was no way to tell
to whom individual bones belonged, this was the place the poet associ-
ated with these ill-fated Korean women.*

Miss ?
You were called *Akemi.*
We don't know your real name,
nor the date or place you died.
We don't know
where your rancor-filled bones
are now buried.

Miss ?
You were a lovely girl,
like a light crimson balsam plant
blooming dreamily,
until that day you were forcibly mobilized
as a "patriotic woman volunteer."

You were despised,
called Korean *P.*

Miss ?
What the men of my country did to you
was to deceive and plunder you,

as if you were not human
but just a cluster of holes.

It was the men of my country,
no longer human,
who became killing penises
growing from the groins of pitiful killer robots.
They attacked you like Japanese swords,
staining your lower belly with blood,
muddying your proud mind
with their soldiers' shoes.

Miss ?
Nights of leaking moonlight and
mornings of blooming azalea,
you were robbed
of even the name your parents gave you.

Afterward you were called *Akemi* and
forced to work for the Great Emperor.
Then on the day the Japanese army fled,
you were abandoned like a rag.

You weren't returned
to your emancipated country,
nor to hateful Japan.

Is your skull buried
even now in a frozen plain?

> *Choui irumun ?*
> > My name is ?
> *Chonum yogie issumnida.*
> > I am here.
> *Chyoruru koguguro toragarusu ikke hejusyo.*
> > Take me to my country.

However hard I listen,
I can't hear your name,
though I can hear fragments of your voice
mixing with the wind.

Who were you?
What was your name?

P—said to have originated from the Chinese word for genital

White Nagasaki
A haiku sequence

Terai Sumie

my child's sleeping face
on this blue earth
radiation everywhere

to the unknown tomorrow
the bomb victims'
prayers turn to sobs

guidepost for the soul
sunflowers that fill
the blue vase

as if
the A-Bomb Maiden incarnate
a dove flies

constant vertigo
still I dread
the White Nagasaki

Talking to Myself

Fukuda Sumako

I have become sick
                of everything.
That huge statue of peace that rises
from the atomic field,
it's OK.
It's OK, but
we can't eat a stone statue,
it cannot fill our real hunger.
Couldn't something else be done with all that money?

And please
don't call me mean.
My state of mind is truthful,
for it is the mind of a survivor,
surviving in the poorest way
all these ten years since the A-bomb.

Ah, yes, this year
I lack energy.
Peace! Peace!
I am tired of hearing about it.
I am exhausted with unreliability
disappearing into deep sky, and
exhausted with fretfulness,
unable to find the answer,
no matter how loud
I yell and cry.

I have become sick of everything.
The more uproarious the people,

the emptier my heart is,
the more sorrow I feel for my dead father,
my dead mother, my dead sister,
all burned to death, and
for their cruel suffering.
So far I have only cried, but now I begin to wonder.
It is they who are happy,
for they need not know all this anxiety and pain that is living.

Oh, I cannot go on like this.
I whip myself, but . . .

Bikini, Be with Hiroshima and Nagasaki

Kurihara Sadako

Uldong,
I hear the waves of Bikini's blue sea
in each spiral shell of your necklace.
It's atoll, like a doughnut,
embraces a small circle of ocean.

Uldong,
this little ocean doesn't have an exit.
It is like the anger and sorrow of your people
before, in broad daylight . . . suddenly, a white flash
flashed on the ocean.
The sun fell, white ash dropped from the dusklike sky,
it fell on the half-naked backs of barefoot adults and children,
and in the cup of coffee the village chief was drinking,
as it fell, its sound was like that of powdery snow on
water towers, on coconut trees, and on the ocean.
The island people, attacked by intense nausea,
vomited until they had no more body fluid.
A torrent of black blood flowed, as if intestines had melted.
Black skin abscessed and people died like burned dogs,
throats grotesquely swollen like toads.

Adults looked like children who had stopped growing.
Dead sperm.
Dead ova.
"Don't eat the coconut or crab!"
"Don't eat the taro!"

The wizards of civilization came to the island,
collected quantities of blood and urine
from reluctant adults and children.

America objected to, suppressed, and hid the islanders' entreaties
to the United Nations,
isolating the island,
making it a guinea pig.
It was the same method used at Hiroshima and Nagasaki,
but it can't be hidden forever.

Uldong,
you came to Hiroshima in the seventeenth year after the A-bomb
from an island far away in the Pacific.

Uldong,
we are the same people of color,
even though our skins are different colors.
That is why we were turned into living experiments.

I hold tightly your unsoiled black hand
        with my yellow hand covered by civilization's dirt.

Uldong — a person who visited Hiroshima from a Pacific island where the U.S.
        had conducted nuclear experiments

tanka

Shoda Shinoe

The black rain falls.
Surely some monster
in the sky has turned over
giant vats
of poison.

Reality
is this and only this—
the one bone
I place in the bent and burned
small school lunch tin.

tanka

Shoda Shinoe

Since
so many small skulls
are gathered here,
these large bones
must be the teacher's.

For the Dead of August

Kurihara Sadako

Let us forge our language
for the dead of August.
No matter how much I speak of "my" details of that day,
it is impossible to speak of Hiroshima.
It is impossible to even talk about the meaning
of a child who burned to death.

Let the dead talk.
Dead,
you must be able to see our lives
better from your side.
Although the chagrin of the dead was carbonized
and remains black and frozen,
the memories of survivors emit a rotten smell
and cannot tell the truth about that day.

The peace writer J. Gartunk says,
> *Hiroshima and Nagasaki were talked about*
> *too much, like an excessive export.*

Hiroshima and Nagasaki were talked about too much,
were worn out and became far distanced from the truth.

Let us forge our language
for the dead of August.
The publishing code of the occupation forces
became a myth,
our language corroded and rusty
with greedy appetites and overtalking.

Let us polish our rasping language and
thrust the anger of the dead
before the ones who manipulate nuclear power.

Hiroshima did not begin the morning of August 6.
It began with the first charge of the Japanese army in Liuyang Lake.
We received the bomb
as the citizens of the army capital, Hiroshima.

Let us remember
Hiroshima exists not only in Hiroshima
but all over the earth.
While the ashes of death swirled the sky,
water, milk, and vegetables were polluted, and
humans became sick
with radioactivity;
don't talk only about "my" details of that day.

Let us freeze the world for a moment
with well-honed, polished language
that pierces the past, present, and future.
Let us make the ones who manipulate nuclear power
turn pallid and halt.

The first time was a mistake,
the second time a betrayal.
Let us not forget our oath to the dead.

haiku

Yamada Setsuko

blowing a breath into the paper crane
gives my electrocardiogram
a blizzard

which cicada-filled tree
answers my questions—
Nagasaki anniversary

in winter milky way
hundreds and thousands of victims
twinkle

haiku

looking for her mother
the girl still has strength
to turn over corpses

Shibata Moriyo

A-bomb anniversary
I am on my way
to till the heavens

Atago Hisayo

a pickled plum
its importance of existence
at the center of explosion

Shibano Sumiko

Sachiko-san, Who Died in the Atomic Bombing

Kurihara Sadako

Iwo Jima fell,
Okinawa died in horror, crushed like a gem stone.
Empty boxes for bones did not return.
The cities burned black.

August 6, 1945,
a quiet sky in deep blue stillness.
Sachiko-san, you, in your air-raid hood,
mobilized people at demolition projects
from which they
were forced to flee.

Suddenly the glowing blue flash,
then crumbling buildings,
flaring flames,
people running,
trying to escape through the tangle
of the fallen power lines,
the swirl of smoke.

On the third night, you came home a corpse,
the dark still unreleased from the
ever howling air-raid warning's shriek.

Hiroshima burned that night without a moon.
That night before defeat,
the whole nation clasped itself in a wakelike state.

Your body lay in a dark room in front of the altar
covered with an air-defense cloth,
a white handkerchief laid by a stranger over your face.

At twilight the injured gone insane
ran through the nearby classrooms yelling like beasts,
while unrecognizable men and women,
swollen like Nioh,
groaned through their burns,
their living bodies reeking of death.

You were at last recognized only by the
iron tag placed on you.
Your corpse lay among rows and rows of corpses
all lined up like rags on the dirt floor of the Koi School,
the white handkerchief
stuck to your burned face.

You, Sachiko-san,
a third-year student of a girls' school,
did not even know the meaning of this war.
Without blooming, you passed away from life,
covered by your mother
with a new flower-patterned *yukata*
over the torn and scorched
air-raid cloth bonded to your skin.

Your mother cried over you,
> *After sewing this, because of the war,*
> *there was not one day when I could*
> *put it on you to wear.*

She then collapsed, crying,
and held you in death.

Nioh — a Buddhist statue, usually ten to fifteen feet tall, used to guard temples
yukata — cotton summer kimono

Evening Primroses

Kurihara Sadako

Evening primroses
the color of pollen
bloomed in the uninhabited city
as if it were a place of falling meteorites.

The city had vanished,
silence passed day and night
over the burned land,
the dead's bones bleached white.
Days passed,
months went by,
then grasses unexpectedly sprouted and
pollen-colored flowers bloomed
like souls of the dead.

An assembly of flowers
on land once an elementary school playground
stuck their stems out of little skulls
and bloomed, stretching between tiny ribs and
small eye sockets.

The crowd of flowers
on the riverbank
blossomed, piling up on each other
from entrails not yet completely
composted into soil.

The flowers sang songs without words
all night long, swaying in the wind,

but together they drooped in the morning
when the time was 8:15 on August 6, 1945.

Neon signs the color of blood
and as numerous as the dead
are shining in the city now, and
evening primroses hardly bloom
anywhere there.

Occasionally at twilight
I happen to glimpse flowers the color of pollen
blooming, scattered
in the hollows of riverbanks and
on the corners of alleys.

tanka

Shoda Shinoe

Every night in her dreams
the mother sees and talks
with her son.
His corpse, even its white bones,
are lost.

Whom
should I ask about
The Last Misery?
I face the total ruins of schoolhouses
and cry.

I wonder
if there is an operation
that removes memories.
Where is a cure
for my pain-filled heart?

A City in Camouflage

Kurihara Sadako

Since then, they have been diligent in hiding the evidence of the crime, have initiated censorship, will not let us utter even a moan. Blocks of the charred city are reorganized; boulevards one hundred meters wide have been built and paved. Green belts are planted with white yucca flowers that bloom each summer. There is a park, and bells toll. High fences enclose the underground construction of tall buildings, and mountains of bones have been buried. They hid everything in the deep pit and then completely camouflaged the city.

Has all the evidence vanished already?
The river delta close to the ocean becomes a tideland at ebb tide, and sometimes white bones can be seen growing on it.

Has all the evidence vanished already?
Have we already lost our memories?

The stone steps in front of the bank imprinted with the shadow of death have been lifted by a crane and placed as if at a funeral in the A-bomb museum.

It is said the bomb victims became monsters, their eyes throwing off strange light, their mouths discharging fire.

These days, with rumors of atomic use in Vietnam common, the Emperor, it is said, has come to pay homage to the cenotaph for the first time.

cenotaph — the A-bomb monument

The Stairs to Heaven
A haiku sequence

Nakao Fusako

on the atomic field
freed doves
the sky scatters radiation

the will of summer
too heavy
for my scarred hands

the atomic field
for my grandchildren
the peaceful time of an afternoon nap

Hiroshima no Pika
A Children's Book (1980)

Maruki Toshi

Hiroshima's sky was bright and clear that morning, its seven rivers flowing. Streetcars ran slowly, and the sun was already glaring down.

Many cities, including Tokyo, Osaka, and Nagoya, had been bombed by planes and burned. But not Hiroshima. "What does this mean?" the people asked. "Will we, too, be attacked?" So they began to prepare, just in case their city was raided. They tore down buildings to widen streets. They made sure there was water along the roads they could use for escape.

All over the city people wore air-raid protection, and each carried a small sack with first-aid supplies.

Mii-chan was at breakfast, eating pink yams with her mother and father. The day before, they had been to the country, where relatives had given them the yams.

Mii-chan, who was very hungry, took a bite. "Oh, this is so delicious," she said in her seven-year-old voice. Her father smiled and agreed, "Yes, they are very good."

At that very moment a terrible white light cut through the sky, shattering the orange morning light, like the light of thousands of thunderbolts striking at once.

But it was not lightning. It was the falling of the atomic bomb. It was the falling of the first atomic bomb on people. It dropped from an American plane, its name, Enola Gay, painted on its side. The bomb itself was named "Little Boy"—such a pretty name for such a terribly awful thing. It fell at 8:15 that morning of August 6, the year of 1945.

Mii-chan woke from unconsciousness to darkness all around her. There was not a sound anywhere. What had happened? She tried to move, but her body wouldn't budge. Then, suddenly, she heard crackling sounds nearby. Red flames jumped up in the dark.

"Fire! Fire!" she heard everywhere.

"Mii-chan, Mii-chan!" her mother's voice called.

With all her might, Mii-chan struggled free of the heavy boards weighing her down. With all her strength she crawled out of a gap in the rubble and ran toward her mother's voice. The mother with tangled hair clasped Mii-chan in her arms.

"Quick, quick! Fire, my dear!" screamed her mother.

They both knew Mii-chan's father was trapped inside.

"He is lost," they cried, pressing their palms together in prayer and facing the terrible fire. Mii-chan's mother saw her husband in the flames, their sounds growing louder each second. Without a word she plunged into the raging fire and dragged him out.

"He has burns all over his body," she sobbed. She took the sash from her kimono and bound it around his body. Then she lifted him onto her back, and with Mii-chan they started to flee.

"Where does she get such strength?" Mii-chan wondered as they ran.

"To the river!" the mother shouted.

"Water!" Mii-chan cried.

When they reached the riverbank, the three of them tumbled in. As they waded out, Mii-chan's hand slipped from her mother's for a moment. Her mother reached for her swiftly. "Be strong," she urged Mii-chan.

Around them were many people chased from their homes by fire. Everywhere faint voices of children were calling, "Water, water." The children's clothes had been burned off, their tender eyelids and tiny lips swollen shut. Many were wandering around, their skin peeled and dangling. With no more strength to go on, some people were lying face down, unable to move. There were people piled on people like small mountains. "Even hell," thought Mii-chan, "could not be more dreadful."

Later, the small family desperately crossed yet another river. There, almost collapsing, her mother put her father down and rested. Something jumped at Mii-chan's feet—a little swallow with burned wings, unable to fly. *Chon, chon.* Corpses and a dead cat came floating down the river.

Mii-chan turned and saw a young woman crying and holding a baby. "I want to feed my baby, but she is already dead," the young mother said to Mii-chan. Then she waded out into deeper water and disappeared into it.

The sky darkened more, and thunder rumbled. It started to rain, a rain black as oil. And even though it was midsummer, there was a chill in the air. Over the dead and injured there appeared a rainbow. A seven-colored rainbow sparkled over everyone.

Mii-chan's mother took Mii-chan's father on her back, and again the three ran. With a fierce force the fire seemed to be following them. They ran over broken tiles, through fallen electric lines and telephone poles, and between row after row of burning houses, until at last they came to another river. Mii-chan was so tired she almost fell asleep in the water. She gulped it in and began to drown. Just in time her mother managed to reach her and Mii-chan was saved.

After what seemed a very long time, Mii-chan and her parents reached Miyajima-guchi. Miyajima Island was dim in a haze of purple. Mii-chan's mother wanted to go to the island by boat. It had many pines and maples and clear water. "The fire can't follow us there," she said. Mii-chan agreed and then closed her eyes. And for the first time since the bomb fell her parents closed their eyes, too.

The sun set. Night came. Day broke. Again night came, then the sun, leading in another morning.

"Excuse me, what day is it?" Mii-chan's mother asked a passerby.

"The ninth," came an answer from a man looking after people who were lying around on the ground.

"Three days," said her mother. "Three days since *Pika*."

Mii-chan began to cry. An old woman, thought to be dead, got up suddenly, took a rice ball from her bundle, and offered it to Mii-chan. It was barley, not rice, Mii-chan noticed. As she took it the woman fell back, not to move again.

"Mii-chan, my dear, you are still holding your chopsticks. Let them go," said her mother in surprise. But the chopsticks would not drop from her hand. Gently, one by one, Mii-chan's mother loosened the fingers that gripped them so tightly. Three days after the bombing the chopsticks finally dropped from Mii-chan's hand.

Firefighters came to help from a nearby village. Soldiers gathered up the dead bodies. The smell of cremation and rotting corpses stifled Mii-chan. Schools that had not burned were turned into hospitals, without beds or sheets. There were no doctors. There was only a building called a hospital where people were laid down on the floor. Mii-chan and her mother took Mii-chan's father inside.

Mii-chan and her mother wondered what had happened to their home. "Let's go and see what it's like where we live," said her mother. When they arrived, they found Mii-chan's rice bowl broken in the rubble. "What has happened to Sa-chan next door and all my other friends?" cried Mii-chan. No one was to be found. Hiroshima had no grass, no trees, not a house as far as one could see. One bomb. It had been only one bomb, but more people than could be counted had already perished. Later many more would also die.

Not only Japanese died. The Koreans who worked as forced laborers died. Their bodies, it is said, were left lying so long that hundreds of crows came to pick at them.

On August 9 a second bomb was dropped on Nagasaki. Many Japanese died there. Many Koreans died there. Some Americans—from the country that dropped the bomb—died as well. Chinese, Russian, and Indonesian people also died from the blasts.

Mii-chan remains as she was at seven, the day of the Flash. She does not grow any bigger. "It is because of *Pika*," her mother says, wiping away tears. When Mii-chan scratches her head and says, "It is itchy," her mother pushes her hair apart tenderly and finds something shiny. With tweezers she pulls out a small piece of glass shattered by *Pika*.

Mii-chan's father was well for a time, even though he had seven wounds. However, one rainy morning the following autumn, his hair fell out, he began bleeding, and he died. Purple spots covered his body.

Some people, grateful for not being injured at the time of the blast, like Mii-chan's father, died later. People who came from other areas looking for friends and relatives died as well. Many injured are still in hospitals, although *Pika* happened thirty-five years ago. Some of them are dying now.

Each year on August 6, Hiroshima's seven rivers are filled with lanterns bearing the names of the *Pika* dead. The names flow down the river on the lighted lanterns to the ocean today as the bodies flowed the day of *Pika*.

Mii-chan wrote two names on her lanterns. One was "Father" and the other was "Swallow."

Today, Mii-chan's white-haired mother pats the head of her daughter who remains forever seven.

"*Pika*," she says, "does not drop. People drop *Pika*."

pika — the A-bomb
chon, chon — the sound of the swallow hopping

To the People Who Make A-Bombs

Fukuda Sumako

You who make A-bombs,
rest your hands a while
and close your eyes.

On the 9th of August
in the year of *Showa,* the year of 20,
the bomb you made took away thousands of lives,
thousands of precious lives.

In one moment, fortunes were nothing,
peaceful homes suddenly and completely destroyed,
their survivors left to start again with nothing but
a desperate life, the fear of no future
due to A-Bomb Disease and limitless sorrow.

You who make A-bombs,
do you ever think of our desperate minds,
of our sorrow that often turns to a curse,
our resignation boiling and turning to anger
each time summer returns?

Think about your invisible hands that
milked the blood of thousands and thousands,
the hands that sold their soul to the devil,
hands that led to ultimate destruction.
We want no more
of your miserable hell.
We do not want any country to taste the evil
your A-bomb brings.

You who make A-bombs
do not want to rest your hands,
saying, they keep the peace.
But look at the sky.
From its beauty, ashes of death approach our heads.

You who make A-bombs,
look at the ocean.
Fish of death are served at tables from
the clean blue sea.
Can there be real world peace
when your hands spread such fear?

It is said,
the Japanese are exaggerating.
Yet is it wrong
for those who know its disaster to speak
seriously about the bomb?

You who make A-bombs,
rest your hands a while and
close your eyes.
If you had experimented with the bomb
in your country,
would you laugh at us now?

It is my parents, my sisters,
my friends who died the cruel death,
their lives less to you than a guinea pig's.
If your bomb brought eternal peace,
I could think of it as a foundation for human existence,
and I would not lament so.

But you who with your hands proceed toward destruction,
march more quickly today than yesterday
and still do not rest your hands.

You who make A-bombs,
abandon without hesitation all you hold in your hands.
Then peace,
true peace, may be born and
humans revive again
as humans.

Fish Talk

Kurihara Sadako

"It's like a heated pool, isn't it?"
"The water is opaque, like a dream."
"I'm so exhausted. I feel like I'm melting!"
"Look, half your tail has dissolved!"
"Atomized kelp and seaweed branches are flowing."
"I see a procession of bones drifting by."
"There, at the bottom of the ocean, cultured shells are rotting."
"We can't see the fishhooks and nets anymore."
"What has happened to the fishermen?"
"I've heard the stamens of purple dayflowers have turned pink."
"Do you think all the humans have died?"
"Did they follow fish to faraway oceans?"
"No, oceans all over the world are getting hotter."
"It's said a Japanese ship with nuclear power was kicked out of
    France."
"The victimized country has become the assailant, hasn't it?"
"Japan a victimized country? You can't be serious!"
"Her coastlines are occupied by white clouds and it's called 'clean
    energy.'"
"They should have built them right in front of the Imperial Palace."
"They wonder if the Emperor, the bent-backed man who used to be
    God, would say, 'A nuclear reactor explosion cannot be avoided.'"
"I'm so tired. I feel like I'm being pulled to the bottom of the
    ocean."
"I can't see."
"Has the ocean turned black?"
"Now it is as dark as a grave, without the slightest trace of light."
"This is it. Good bye. . . ."

Untitled Childhood Recollection

Kubo Shizuko
eight years old in 1945

My sister and I were in the air-raid shelter. My mother had just gone to the field to get cucumbers when the horrible Flash shined in. After that there was a loud, rumbling sound outside the shelter. Shrinking with fear, I lay down on my stomach. But I was so worried about my mother that I crawled over to peek outside.

Flames were raging from the windows of every building at the nearby university. It was astonishing. Everything looked completely different than it had the minute before.

I could not help thinking that I had wandered into another world.

I began to cry in fear and helplessness. Without my realizing it, my legs were climbing the hill and I was crying, "Mom! Mom!"

I ran to a neighbor I knew well. She comforted me and kindly took me to her house. I could not stop feeling that my mother was calling "Shizuko!" somewhere. Because of fear I did not allow myself to look for her. Finally I could not stand it anymore and asked the neighbor to come with me to the cucumber field. There, I again thought I heard my mother's voice faintly calling my name.

Near the narrow side of the road was a big rock. We saw someone lying by it and I recognized the *monpe* pattern. "Mom," I cried and ran to her, but she did not answer.

Blood was flowing all over, and my mother's face was completely deformed.

I just stood there, absentmindedly looking at her corpse. It was too horrible for me to understand. I shed no tears, felt no sorrow or any other feeling.

She must have been thrown by the blast, hitting her head on the rock.

Ten days later my father died from radiation.

At that time I became like an imbecile, not even crying.

I think about my father and mother a lot these days, and each time I am so full of sorrow that I cry and cry. . . . If I had shed tears then, would they have survived?

I just can't help thinking this way. . . .

monpe —traditional Japanese trousers

haiku

Kingyo Humiko

grabbing sand
beneath the flaming sky
is to be alive

under scorching sun
we step over corpses
like jumping over ditches

crows fly down
that corpse doesn't have
its head

I Witness Hiroshima

Kurihara Sadako

I, a survivor, wish
above all to be human.
Especially as a mother
I object above all to war
when over the red cheeks of children and all others
there hangs a blue sky ready one day to be torn up suddenly,
executing all their futures by fire.

I pour my tears over the living rather
than the potential corpses, and I object
more than anything to war.

If a mother's rejection of her own children's deaths
is punished by some horrible name,
on my eyes are printed that day's horror
from which I do not run or hide.

On August 6, 1945,
soon after the sun began to shine,
people humbly began their day.
Then suddenly the city was blown away and
its seven rivers filled with the bodies of the dead.

There is a tale about the devil that says
if we catch a glimpse of hell and speak of it,
we are pulled back to hell,

and I, who witness for Hiroshima,
witness wherever I go.
I, who survived, sing with all my being
for all to hear:
      "Let war stop, now."

Bright, Vivid, and Creative:
The Women's Peace Movement in Hiroshima and the Delta Women's Group

Yamaguchi Misao, 1991

The Delta Women's Group has been in existence for ten years. Ordinary women connected by one thought, "no war," have been using creative methods to voice this idea whenever possible. I would like to introduce our movement, which continues to be active, though we are often called "willful show-offs of Delta" and "always-eating Delta" (since we often bring snacks to meetings!).

The Birth of the Delta Women's Group

On March 21, 1982, a peace action of 200,000 people was held in the Hiroshima Peace Memorial Park under the swelling buds of cherry blossoms. On that day, women from twenty-four grassroots groups distributed leaflets with the message, "No war! Let us build a viable women's movement." Then we sat in a circle on five straw mats in one corner of the park.

A single woman in her fifties said, "I met *Pika* thirty-seven years ago. Since then I've been holding the bomb inside my body, wondering when it will explode. . . . I'm absolutely against nuclear weapons and war."

"I'm a divorced single mother," said another. "Now I can't help getting mad at the government. The military budget increases, and the social welfare budget decreases. Officials say, 'Civilians can exist as the goverment exists.' But they should say, 'A government can exist as civilians exist.'"

"We do not need one cent for the military budget," said a woman in her forties.

We all gave witness to our thoughts, one by one, speaking into a microphone at times and becoming inspired by our own words. Passersby and others who read our leaflets joined in, sometimes in twos or threes.

"I became frightened about the direction of our society ever since my second child was born. Before that I was preoccupied with being a 'good mother,' but I realized that wasn't enough. So I have come to join you, to look for something I can do for my children's future," said a homemaker.

The circle of women who spoke grew larger, and the discussion became very active as passersby offered their opinions.

Around this time, in 1982, antinuclear movements were spreading vigorously in Europe and in the United States. In Europe demonstrations and protest meetings, each with hundreds of thousands of people, took place to protest the impending installation of Pershing II mid-distance nuclear cruise missiles. This wave of protest was coming to Japan.

The Delta Women's Group was born with those one-minute speeches in the Peace Memorial Park. Through their actions and in their own words they were pleading antiwar, antinuclear-power, as well as antimissile sentiments. The group included women from their twenties to their sixties—homemakers, working women, single women, unmarried partners, and divorced women. The range of the women's jobs was also diverse—office workers, beauticians, teachers, civil servants, counselors, and others.

At first we didn't know what to do, even though each of us wanted to act. To begin with, we went to inspect the American navy base in Iwakuni. We also organized various events, such as posting handmade signs saying, "No military budget! Use your vote!" during the local general election time. We arranged a gathering of A-bomb survivors and sponsored protests against Japan's 200-million-dollar military budget.

In Europe the flame of antinuclear feeling was raging more vigorously than ever before. For two years women had been setting up tents in front of the British military base in Greenham Commons as a bold, nonviolent direct action of protest against the installation of nuclear cruise missiles. In October 1983 three women in the Delta Group felt a great desire and need to meet with the women in Greenham. Meeting these women who were conducting a creative, autonomous, and nonviolent antinuclear movement with singing, dancing, and talking, even in freezing weather and amid police harassment, gave great impetus to the Delta Women's Group.

Women Leave Home for Peace

In the summer of 1984 Hiro Sumpter, the only Japanese person still working at the peace camp at Greenham, visited Japan. Hiro interacted with twenty-one grassroots groups from Hokkaido to Okinawa. Hiro was a guest at a gathering of the lively and bold Women's Antinuclear Action in Hiroshima. "Women should have confidence in themselves. Women must trust women," she told us. Hiro's words echoed deeply in our hearts.

In 1985, 203 women from Niigata to Oita met for the "August 6 Women's Gathering in Hiroshima." The gymnasium designated for the meeting was decorated with colorful hand-made banners, brought by the women. The place was filled with the energy of those women—singing, talking, laughing, and getting angry. One of the members of Delta wrote, "Those women seemed very familiar to me. It was a heartfelt meeting with women who had been rejecting the oppression in their daily lives and who continued to be angry without giving up."

On April 26, 1986, the accident at the Chernobyl nuclear plant in the Soviet Union occurred. Our surprise and anger were tremendous. One of the Delta members wrote, "It was such a shock to imagine that my milk, which my youngest one drinks, also is tainted by radiation. My susceptible daughter and I just hugged each other and cried." A citizens' group entitled, "Let's Not Repeat Hiroshima and Chernobyl. Express Your Voices, Now!" met on June 15. The next day nine protesters from Delta stormed the Chugoku Electric Power Company saying, "We're afraid to breast-feed our babies. Please stop the nuclear power plant immediately. We don't mind dying, because we have been able to live until today in spite of the A-bomb, but we want our daughters to live full lives." Delta then began supporting the movements against building nuclear power plants in other regions.

At the "Let's Not Repeat Hiroshima and Chernobyl" meeting our modest suggestions to place the panelists' chairs on the same level as the participants and to write a poem as a declaration met strong resistance from the male members of the committee. A large gap opened between the men, who had reservations about the form of the meeting, and us, and we felt a sense of deep exhaustion.

In 1987 we held the "August 6 Women's Gathering in Hiroshima," hoping this women-only gathering would re-energize us. One hundred fifty women from around the nation came to take part. One member, whose husband had been unsupportive in the beginning and had called his wife selfish, now says, "My husband has become very cooperative with my activities of the past five years."

The Delta Women's Group remains active and is involved in local and national issues to express its consistent "no war, no nuclear war, no nuclear power plant" sentiments.

Continuous Prayers #15

Ishikawa Itsuko

I hear
I hear
> *Kimiga-yo-wa-*
> *chiyoni-yachiyoni*
> *sazare-ishino-*

Who is singing?
Is it Sato-san floating burned down the river?
Matsuki-san?
Arakawa-sensei?

> *Iwaoto narite*
> *koke-ne*

No, no,
it is the voices of healthy children
fifty years after
the A-bomb fell.

Do you know the meaning of the song?
Do you know the enormous quantity
of blood, of Asian children's blood, that
spilled with that song?

Do you know us
burned, sunk in agony,
hands released from floating wood
unable to finish the song?

koke no
mu-su-ma-de-

I don't want to listen
ever again to that song,
never again that song.

Don't make me listen,
please don't!
Even though I became
only bones rattling on the river
it gives me unbearable pain.
Don't sing that song.
Please—
never sing that song.

Kimigayo—Japanese national anthem

Continuous Prayers #20

Ishikawa Itsuko

I want to go home
I want to go home
because I am only bones
all the more
I want to go home

I want to go to my hometown
where azaleas bloom as far as I can see
I want to go home
crossing the Sea of Genkai

I don't want cars to run over me
I don't want great crowds of Japanese to step on me
at the hundred-meter-wide boulevard
because I am only bones

All the more
I want to go back silently
to my grassy hillside home
I want to go back quietly and
listen to bird songs

I am not a number
not just a figure
even if I am bones

I am a human
and want to go back home
crossing the Sea of Genkai
because I am bones
all the more
I want to go home

Continuous Prayers #24

Ishikawa Itsuko

I wonder
how many hundreds of bodies I piled in the truck?
How could I have had time to hold each one gently?
It was like lifting torn sacks,
picking up their intestines with a pick,
raising them up, throwing them into the truck bed.

They stank unbearably.
It was especially hard when they crumbled to the ground, and
I tried to scoop them up with my shovel.
Melted eyeballs, severed black
arms on the earth.

I am telling you, only you, what
I have never told anyone.

All the time I was breathing radioactivity.
Does my breath stink?
Tell me, please, honestly.

The dead souls were stinking, but
it wasn't I who killed them —
it wasn't I.

But I can't feel I am without sin,
leveling piles of the dead
as if they were a mountain of gravel,
stabbing them with a pick
to throw them away.

Even corpses have the right
to be treated respectfully.

I think my sin cannot be erased
because I was a soldier or
because I was given an order.

I am telling only you this.
I will die soon,
ruined by radioactivity produced by the fission
of uranium atoms.

I want to tell only you.
For some reason I want to tell you
what I have been holding inside myself.
Is it to put my sin on you?
I cannot die in silence.

The dead could not be called human anymore,
their skins peeled,
their bodies crumbled and melted,
their legs and arms like stiff, burned sticks.
They must have been eating a second bowl of
green-leaf soup, or combing their hair, or singing songs
that very morning.

You know
they were like barbecued chicken,
and I lifted them with the pick,
scooped them with the shovel,
their black human grease shed stagnant on the street.
This is what the thing called
uranium did.

Do I stink?
I know I do.
I am the same as those dead.
Oh, that thing called uranium . . .
even after eighteen years.

I can't see
        . . . can't see.

Continuous Prayers #29

Ishikawa Itsuko

Mother, you have become so small and thin.
The grave you pray to does not hold my bones.
They are not in the grave looking out over the ocean.
If only I had a hand I would write to you.
If only I had a mouth I would call to you:
> *Hello, hello.*
> *I'm in Florida, at Rick's house.*

Among a broken toaster, a rusty bicycle, the deserted shoes of soldiers, a moldy backpack, I lay in the starless night. I was secretly
dug from the Ninojima trench, polished up as much as it was possible, and put on the souvenir shop shelf where Rick bought me.

> *Hey, Maria!*
> *Look, a Jap's skull*
> *after we nuked it!*

For a while I was a decoration in a cabinet at their home but
soon abandoned to the storeroom.

The Florida summer passes,
then another and another,
now Rick and Maria are an old couple with grandchildren.

The same age as Maria, torched by America, I am now only a skull.
Today I lie down
in that America.

Mother, over eighty years old,
you have become so small and thin.
My bones are not in the grave you pray to.

> *Hello, hello.*
> *I'm in Florida, at Rick's house.*

Ninojima — a small island in the Hiroshima bay

tanka

Shoda Shinoe

Behind the Jizoson,
its head blown away
by the bomb,
cosmos drop their seed
then wither.

Isn't it strange—
Japanese rearmament?
Even though
we vowed never to repeat
our mistake again.

Jizoson—stone Buddha sculpture

tanka

Shoda Shinoe

Pika don!
After
the silence
I opened my eyes.
The scene had turned to carnage
and deadly moans.

Lady! Lady!
A totally burned body
called out to me.
Red and
split like a pomegranate.

Pika don — the sound the A-bomb made

Requiem for a Korean Girl

Ishikawa Itsuko

Does the ocean remember a girl
quietly staring at the dark waves
from the night deck of a cargo ship
more than forty years ago?

A ship headed straight toward the south.
       I want to become a fish.
       I want to become a bird.
       I wish I would become even a small fruit so that I
       could float and reach my beloved country.
The girl's thought was headed straight north.
Omoni!

My mother's eyes must be swollen from looking so long for me.
       There is no way to tell you . . .
       how, bringing ceremonial rice cakes
       to my great uncle,
       I was caught by a truckload of Japanese soldiers,
       threatened by their guns and
       brought right to the ocean
       where I am now.
       Soon I realized
       the meaning of the headband with the word
         "volunteer"
       that they forced me to put on
       so they could brutalize me.

In southern islands
lines of soldiers are waiting for you.

But before, here in the ship,
him and him and him and they . . .

   I am staring at the blue-black ocean,
   dragging the chain around my feet.
   Uenom!

   I will never allow you to plunder my body
   even after you have taken my country, my language,
      as well as my name.

   I would rather be eaten by a fish in the dark
   than give up.

   Fish, eat me,
   with all my tears.
   Swim straight to the north,
   to the shore of my hometown
   and be caught in the net of *aboji!*

   Fish, if you won't go,
   bird, oh, bird,
   peck my soul rising from the bottom of the ocean.
   Fly away to the north.
         To the north!

   Perch in the bamboo forest
   behind the house I love,
   utter a single song, *omoni!*

   I cannot stay here any longer.
   Let me find a grave in the water
   with my pure mind
   with my pure body
   before they find me.

So long, so long—

Did fish eat the girl,
so precious to her parents,
who sank down in the dark sea?

Did a bird really peck her soul?

Ocean,
do you know the whereabouts
of this girl's remains?

omoni—mother
uenom—beastly Japanese
aboji—father

Hiroshima Being Questioned
Excerpts

Kurihara Sadako, 1991

The government and public figures often say that Japan was the only country attacked by the A-bomb. Yet it was not the nation, but people—including women, children, and the elderly—who were victimized by the A-bomb. Not only Japanese people but many foreigners suffered from it as well. Among the foreigners Koreans received the most exposure. It is said that about 70,000 Koreans were affected by the A-bomb. The Korean survivors ask the Japanese why it was that they were involved and victimized in another country's war.

After the annexation of Korea by Japan in 1910 and its subsequent colonization, Korean people were taken from their land, deprived of their language, and made to take Japanese names.

The importance of Hiroshima has expanded from the early stage of revealing the misery of the A-bomb to allowing discussion of issues surrounding the nuclear civilization that produced the bomb and widening the point of view concerning the destruction of humanity, the earth, and the environment. This view demands that Japan take responsibility for the militarism that led to the invasion of Asian neighbors, war with the United States, and ultimately the A-bomb.

We are now forming networks of nuclear radiation victims, said to be eighteen million worldwide. These networks assist the victims of Semipalatinsk and Chernobyl and offer them medical information.

The National Responsibility for War and the Victims of Nuclear Radiation
Excerpts

Kurihara Sadako, 1985

Many politicians, whether conservative or reformed, emphasize that Japan is the only country to have suffered the A-bomb. Japan, however, is not the only country to have experienced nuclear damage.

Victims of nuclear experiments in the Pacific Ocean protest, saying that since World War II some two hundred nuclear blasts have been documented there. They cannot be called experiments. They were nuclear war itself, because many people died and many still suffer from radiation sickness. Yet Japan declares itself the only country to have suffered nuclear damage, refusing to recognize how far its responsibility reaches.

In the United States, which dropped the A-bomb, one million people were exposed to excessive radiation. This number includes 750,000 civilians who were at the sites of nuclear experiments, nuclear factories, and uranium mining. It includes the accident at Three Mile Island and the 250,000 veterans who participated in experimental nuclear maneuvers in Nevada and on Bikini Island.

In England, too, 10,000 veterans were exposed to radiation during nuclear experiments in Australia and Christmas Island in the 1950s. Some of them died from leukemia, and various post-exposure symptoms have appeared in their children. The Australian government has begun health checks on the 15,000 military personnel and aboriginal people who were exposed to excessive radiation during England's nuclear experiments there.

People who have been exposed to radiation have broken through the thick wall of press control to report their existence in the former U.S.S.R. and China.

Japan cannot survive this nuclear age by declaring it is the only country to have suffered nuclear damage.

The War Experience and Literature
Excerpts

Kurihara Sadako, 1981

At the A-Bomb Memorial Monument, in February 1981, Pope John Paul II made an appeal to the world. He emphasized repeatedly that to be responsible for the future we have to look back at the past. Talking about our own war experiences means exactly that: taking responsibility for our future. Today, however, it is impossible for any one person to capture the experience of contemporary war, especially if it is a nuclear war. Since both enemy and ally are destroyed there are no survivors to relate their experiences.

A few days after the A-bomb was dropped on Hiroshima, I walked around the ruins of the Second Unit of the West Region in Kamiya-cho, half a kilometer from the center of the explosion. Numerous burned-red iron helmets were lying on the ground with debris all around them. Human bodies, like broiled fish with white bones, were on simple iron-frame beds in the army hospital.

War first begins with the declaration of a state of emergency. The government makes a secret protection law, so that it can thoroughly suppress freedom of speech. Then it starts a war under these conditions of secrecy and restricted freedom. According to a national mobilization law, scientists, engineers, doctors, nurses, and even people like carpenters and plasterers are forcibly drafted into the military.

In the last war everyone, military and civilian alike, was mobilized to build war plants and air-raid shelters and to do farming and evacuation work. Lands were forcibly expropriated for military roads and positions. Everything, including food, was taken away for the war. At the last, people were made to sacrifice even metal Buddhist house shrines and gold wedding rings.

People were forced into lives of extreme privation—without

food, without clothes, without a doctor or medicine during illness.

Furthermore, if people mentioned the slightest complaint or discontent about conditions, they were immediately threatened and harassed as disloyal traitors and rebels. Children were constantly hungry and never saw any candy. An exhaustive education of Emperor worship was enacted in the schools. Before eating their lunch of food formerly fed to pigs, children recited, "We were born for His Imperial Majesty and will gladly die for His Imperial Majesty. Even if only a grain of rice is given to us by His Imperial Majesty, we will never waste it." Since all of the coercion during wartime was done in the Emperor's name, our war experiences are inseparably tied to fear of the Emperor.

As the war proceeded, people were exposed to air raids and bombardments. Their houses and possessions were burned; families died or were injured. Many war orphans roamed the burned ruins like street urchins.

In Okinawa, people were not only attacked by the American army, but they were also robbed of food and their air-raid shelters destroyed by the military of their own country. There were even cases in which crying babies were stabbed and killed by the swords of Japanese soldiers for fear of being discovered by the American army. In the end, people were made to commit group suicides. Consequently, there is now a very strong anti-militarist movement against the Japanese Self-Defense Force and the American army in Okinawa.

When the A-bomb was dropped on Hiroshima and Nagasaki, 300,000 citizens died. Even now, 400,000 survivors are suffering from post-A-bomb symptoms and from fear.

The survivors are demanding passage of an aid law requiring governmental compensation based on the state's responsibility for the war. In response, the government's A-bomb committee said that since the damages were suffered during a national emergency, everyone should equally endure the hardships. This means not only that the government exempts itself from responsibility for the war but also that the government will be engaged in wars in the future and will impose sacrifices on its citizens. Survivors and others are indignant that a government impudently forces people to sacrifice in spite of a peace constitution. This indignation has resulted in frequent meetings and declarations of protest.

Dropping the A-bomb was an inhuman act violating international law. At the same time we should never forget that it was dropped at the end of fifteen years of war, brought on as the miserable result of Japanese imperialism's invasion of Asia. Hiroshima and Nagasaki in particular became victims of the national policy of Emperorism.

The Allied nations issued the Potsdam Declaration on July 26, 1945, and sent an ultimatum of unconditional surrender with a deadline of August 3. The Japanese government ignored this ultimatum, however, declaring that there would be no surrender if the Allies did not allow Japan to retain the national policy of Emperorism. If the Japanese government had accepted the Potsdam Declaration by August 3, the victims of Hiroshima and Nagasaki would have been spared. The people in Hiroshima and Nagasaki were victims not only of the A-bomb America dropped, but also of Emperorism.

Though we are A-bomb survivors, at the same time we belonged and still belong to the country that perpetrated and continues to perpetrate invasion of Asian countries; therefore, we cannot be exempt from our responsibility as perpetrators of war. Asian people often say, "Since Japan was A-bombed on August 6 and 9, 1945, she forgot her war responsibility as a perpetrator." Korean people say, "The A-bomb liberated us from thirty-five cruel years of Japanese imperialism. Japanese imperialism is more awful than the A-bomb." Also, Southeast Asian people say that if A-bombs had been dropped not only on Hiroshima and Nagasaki but also on Tokyo and Osaka, Japan would have been totally destroyed and they would not be receiving today's terrible economic invasions. They are very afraid of Japan's rearming and militarism, expecting militaristic invasion along with the economic invasion.

Furthermore, the Japanese government recently agreed with the policy of the United States to dump nuclear waste in the Pacific Ocean and to construct, with the cooperation of the Japanese Self-Defense Force, storage sites on U. S. military bases on Pacific islands. Joint maneuvers between Japan and the United States have already begun. How can we mention Hiroshima, Nagasaki, A-bomb survivors, or demilitarized neutrality while we allow the rearmament of our own country and the dumping of nuclear waste in the ocean?

In schools today, though, national defense, our anthem, *Kimigayo,* and the Rising Sun Flag are part of the curriculum conscientious educators are teaching about the A-bomb and war experiences to students who don't know about the war. The Education Ministry, boards of education, and parents who are concerned about the quality of the universities accuse those teachers of bias. Nevertheless, these teachers are committed to peace education, determined not to repeat the mistakes of history by sending schoolchildren to the battlefields.

All students must become educated about past militarism. We must focus on our war experiences to change the direction of politics, education, culture, and society and to proceed toward the creation of peace under the fortress of our constitution, which declares the abandonment of war.

haiku

an arm
severed by the blast
its hand grabs midsummer soil

Yonemura Chikuko

I want to shake
the stone absorbing summer heat,
listen to its voice

Endo Toshiko

the boy smiles
bites into a tomato
becomes a corpse

Shibata Moriyo

haiku

on the burned field
an orange-crate casket
one leg sticking out

Atago Hisayo

A-bomb anniversary
the colors of the thousand paper cranes
fade each year

Murakami Mineko

there is my missing brother
melted into a
museum panel

Mochita Ritsuko

We Must Doubt as well as Trust

Yamaoka Michiko

From a talk to Japanese students on a field trip to Hiroshima in which the speaker told of her experience when the A-bomb was dropped and of the kindness of Quakers who helped her receive treatment in the United States.

When you got off the train, you thought Hiroshima looked like a tourist spot, didn't you? You must have wondered where the A-bomb was dropped. Things age and weather, and the city planned to clean up the disgrace of this river. Shame on them.

A lot of people died after jumping into the river because there was no place else to flee. High tide came and their corpses flowed to the ocean. But roof tiles blown into the river by the blast were heavy and sank, so there were many tiles there. Hearing the river was to be cleaned, high-school students dug them out, and those very tiles were used to build this monument.

Five-thousand-degree heat burned these tiles—and my hand. I feel pain in it now if it is pinched, but I didn't feel anything when my hand was once bitten by a mosquito and bled. I knew it only after my friend told me.

People, as well as roof tiles, were all burned black.

When I was struck by the A-bomb I was fifteen years old, two years older than you. Thinking back, young people then trusted what adults said, what the government said, never doubting any of their words. It's important for us to doubt as well as trust. I survived the A-bomb. It changed my life. It's been seven years since I decided to tell my story to children. The first time I spoke in front of students I felt such pain because I didn't want to remember. But if I don't tell my story, nobody will understand that this peace didn't come easily. I tell it not because I want your sympathy, but because I want you to build a world with no war.

As soon as I entered middle school in 1943, we had to change our skirts to *monpe* "to protect the nation." In gym class we built straw dolls on the playground and stabbed them with bamboo spears, pretending they were enemies. The following year, we were mobilized to work in local governmental jobs at the central telephone department or savings department and such. There were no Sundays, no holidays. Our lunch was porridge or potatoes. We just followed the order to work for the nation, with no chance to use our own judgment.

On August 6, in the early morning, I was walking toward the central telephone department, where I worked as an operator. It was five hundred meters away from the center of the coming explosion. The sun was scorching already, and there wasn't a cloud in the sky.

I heard the faint sound of an airplane and looked up, shading my eyes with my right hand. At that moment the Flash came, knocking me unconscious. My face grew puffy. The Flash was a beautiful bluish yellow color, and when I regained consciousness, I found myself stuck between stones. Somewhere voices were calling for help, but I couldn't move or utter a word. I heard the sound of crackling fire. The flash of five thousand degrees set wooden things on fire. "Help me, Mom! Help!" I finally screamed. Then I heard my mother's voice, "Michiko! Michiko!" She was looking for me. I thought I was going to die. My mother, who had been under the house, crawled out and came to look for me. But the stone on top of me was too heavy for her to lift. Finally, I was rescued by a soldier.

What I saw after that was hell in this world. There was no one who looked like a human being. There were no normal faces. The skin of my hands was peeled and hanging down. I couldn't see what my face was like. There were people whose entrails were hanging from their bodies, people without legs, and people who couldn't utter a sound, their bodies and clothes burning. I couldn't help the children who were asking for help, calling out, "Give me water!" "Where can I flee?" "Help me!" My mother told me I would have to escape to a safe place by myself because she had to look for my cousins.

People, their entrails exposed, fled like ghosts in a direction away from fire. Some people tried to put their entrails back into their bodies. That's why even now I can't eat a sausage.

I was placed down on the ground after we arrived at Hiji Mountain. It was scorchingly hot. Flies swarmed on us and maggots hatched. The first medicine I got was tempura oil. I now know that the military had plenty of provisions, although we ordinary people didn't have any oil or sugar at home.

After the tempura oil, I felt pain for the first time, and the skin on my face collapsed. I couldn't see anything. I thought that I would die on the spot. But a miracle happened. My mother found me again.

I really don't want you ever to experience the suffering I had to go through then and long afterwards.

My mother and I were sent to a refugee camp on an island. There people died constantly, and the corpses were piled up, doused with gasoline, and burned. I recovered six months later but my neck remained stuck to my left shoulder and three fingers of my right hand were fused together. My mother rubbed the scars on my hands desperately. I used to wonder when she ever slept, because whenever I woke up in the middle of the night, I always found her hands rubbing my scars.

My father died when I was four years old and my mother raised me, working as a day laborer or doing night jobs.

Because of my disfigured face, people often threw stones at me and mocked me, saying, "A monster is coming!" We went back to my mother's hometown, but, seeing my red, swollen scars, our relatives said, "How awful! It must be contagious. Leave at once!" The A-bomb had even destroyed people's minds.

We came back to Hiroshima, which was a field of burned ruins. We ate the first grains that grew in Hiroshima without knowing that they contained radiation. We tilled the soil, contaminated with radiation, planted vegetables, and ate them.

My scars finally got better, and I applied for jobs but I was always turned down: "We can't hire you because of your face."

After the war, those who had money couldn't use it because of the economic blockade. The only food distributed was a quarter of a mackerel and one *go* of rice a day per household. We couldn't talk about the A-bomb because of press censorship by the American occupation army. And our government didn't do anything to help us.

In 1952 Japan was released from American occupation. We were free to say anything and peace movements started. People in Tokyo invited survivors for medical treatment. But there was a limit because we were all poor.

Before Japan's emancipation, an American journalist, Norman Cousins, organized support for our treatment in the United States. It was not the U. S. government but a Quaker group that invited us—about eighty women with bent hands or scars or without hair—to the United States. It took three years of treatment for my neck to return to its original position and each finger to separate from the others. My face had thirty-seven operations, using the skin from other parts of my body. That was in 1955.

In America the people said to us, "We are very sorry that our nation did this terrible thing to you." Then I realized that they knew the war had been wrong, and I was able to forgive them. I realized that if people communicated with their hearts, no war could occur. On my way to the United States I was afraid of America, but on the way back I regained my laughter.

After my mother died nine years ago, I developed cancer. I thought, "It is perhaps time for me to die." When I was about to jump off the roof of the hospital, I remembered what my mother had said to me, "You must live on, Michiko." It's been five years since then, and the cancer hasn't metastasized.

Now I think we should never forget what happened. Never. I am sure it's my duty as a survivor to convey the truth to all of you for the sake of my friends who died in front of my eyes.

monpe—traditional Japanese trousers
go—a measure a little less than a cup

When We Say "Hiroshima"

Kurihara Sadako

When we say, "Hiroshima,"
is the response a gentle, "Ah, Hiroshima"?

When we say, "Hiroshima,"
the response is, "Pearl Harbor."
When we say, "Hiroshima,"
the response is, "Nanking Massacre."
When we say, "Hiroshima,"
the response is, "The Manila Fire Stake," where Japanese
    troops locked women and children in trenches, soaked them
    with gasoline, and burned them.
When we say, "Hiroshima,"
echoes of blood and flames come back to us.

When we say, "Hiroshima,"
the response is not a gentle, "Ah, Hiroshima,"
as innocent dead Asians belch out anger at their assault.

For the gentle response, "Ah, Hiroshima,"
we would have to abandon our weapons as we were supposed
    to do,
we would have to get rid of the foreign military bases in Japan.

Until that day,
Hiroshima will remain a city embittered by cruelty and distrust.
We will remain a pariah scorched by latent radioactivity.

For the gentle response, "Ah, Hiroshima,"
we must first cleanse our soiled hands.

Flag

Kurihara Sadako

The red of the Rising Sun is people's blood,
its background of white is people's bones.

The flag of blood and bone
was hoisted in every war
where it drained the blood
and made bones
of other countries' women and children.

When the wars were over,
it became the flag of peace
hoisted high at Olympic and Asian tournaments.

Whenever Japan wins a victory,
Kimigayo is played, and the
flag of crime
which sucked the blood and exposed the bones
of ten million people
flies shamelessly with

> *Kimiga-yo-wa*
>> *May the reign of the Great Emperor*
> *chiyoni-yachiyoni*
>> *last forever and age until pebbles become*
> *koke no-mu-su-ma-de*
>> *rocks covered with moss*

Because of it,
people spilled their blood and
exposed their bones,

bones not yet returned and
bones left in the fields and mountains of Asia.

However,
have we already forgotten about
the bones in Wan Ren Keng, China,
bones deserted in southern islands,
having eaten soybean dregs, grasshoppers,
taro leaves, yet hungry,
infested with lice at group evacuation centers and
taken from their mothers,
whole families holding their breath in air-raid shelters,
the dark nights filled with air-raid alarms,
300,000 people burned dead by the Flash—
have we already forgotten all of those?

The flag of blood and bone flies every night
forever accompanied by *Kimigayo*.
When all the TV programs are over,
people's day is completed by raising the Rising Sun flag.
It flies on the rooftops of city halls, over playgrounds, over schools,
and in the sky above the monument
in Peace Memorial Park
as if nothing had ever happened.

The red of the Rising Sun is people's blood,
its background of white is people's bones.
People of Asia never forget,
even though the Japanese do.

Kimigayo—Japanese national anthem
Wan Ren Keng—literally "holes with thousands of people in them," indicating
                the mass graves of those killed in the Nanking massacre

78

The A-Bomb Disease I Didn't Know

Park Cha Jom

I was born in Japan and lived in Hiroshima because my father had been forced to come to Japan.

My father, who died eighteen years ago, would be eighty-four years old if he had lived. His birthplace, which should be my real hometown, is in a rural area of Korea called Sachon, close to Kyongsan. When I went to my liberated mother country, it was with resentment, because I wondered why my parents had abandoned such a beautiful, peaceful hometown to lead a humiliating life in Japan.

But I came to understand the situation better as the years passed.

Japanese people, especially those over fifty years old, must remember the annexation of Korea by Japan from 1910 to 1945. All Japanese were made aware of the unification of Korea and Japan.

According to my father, young people in Korea at that time had been continuously urged to leave their hometowns or villages and to go to Japan or Manchuria, under the slogan of "Reclamation." My father was one of them. He was a farmer and chose to go to Japan, where his cousin was already in Kanagawa prefecture. He was thirty-one years old at the time.

I was born in Yokohama City. My father worked for a company and I looked forward to having a monthly feast on his paydays.

Before long, influenced by our Hiroshima relatives' suggestions, we moved there, where life seemed a little bit easier. I graduated and went to nursing school at a hospital, where I worked as an assistant nurse.

Around 8 A.M. on August 6, 1945, I was walking in the

corridor with patients and saw something coming down from the sky and spinning around. I thought it must be leaflets because, in those days, they were scattered from airplanes almost every day.

At that instant, a ray like lightning flashed. I was thrust down to the ground by a tremendous clattering sound. I heard screams for help everywhere. I was knocked unconscious.

I didn't know how much time passed. When I opened my eyes, a soldier was shaking my body vigorously. He told me a fire was coming that way and I should flee immediately, but I could not get up. My head was bloody and reeling. My left leg was bleeding and swollen. The soldier carried me outside on his back.

It was wretched and miserable beyond imagination outside, as if it were another world. People were roaming around like monsters, stretching out their hands for water. I saw schoolgirls jump headfirst into the water tanks reserved for fighting fires. An army truck filled with the injured came by and two soldiers helped me get on. Everyone was half-insane, crying, "The airplane will come again!"

We were taken to a pier, which I found out later was the navy school in Etajima. Many victims of the A-bomb were already gathered there. Burned people died one after another. Some just babbled insanely. I was scared to death.

Someone at the treatment center recommended amputating my swollen leg. I said, "No!" and tried to treat it myself with Mercurochrome and a tincture of iodine. Injured and bleeding, people lying beside me were dying painfully, maggots hatching in their burns. I felt as if I were dead, too, and couldn't eat the rice balls that were distributed. I just waited for my parents. Nobody came. I assumed everyone in my family had been killed.

Several days passed. Then one day, when I was wondering what I should do, my sister, Masako, came looking for me. She was really dirty and brought many rice balls with her. We were so glad to be alive and talked and cried together. She said that my family had fled and was staying on a straw mat under the Yokokawa bridge. Since I could not walk, I asked someone to carry me in exchange for some of our rice. Eventually we arrived at the place to which my family had fled.

On the day of the A-bomb, there were five family members at home: my parents; my younger brother, Suboku; my younger sister, Masako; and an older sister who was pregnant and visiting at that time. Another brother and sister had been mobilized.

Suboku was parching beans. When the substitute meal for wheat flour was ready, the Flash came. Suboku stood up, shouting, "Mother!" and the whole house crumbled and fell. It became pitch dark; he shouted, "Mother! Mother!"

"I'm here!" my mother said, trying to get out, holding him, but there was no exit. Then my father called out, and they found a gap in the crumbled house and crawled out.

They fled under the bridge, not knowing the whereabouts of my brother and sister. My father looked for them in vain. My mother got very angry, crying, "The dirty Japanese killed my children."

On the seventh day, my brother, filthy and black, came to the bridge with my father. How glad my mother was! Only one, my sister, was still missing.

On August 15 we heard of Japan's unconditional surrender. Finally we were independent after so much humiliation. Several days later we moved to an acquaintance's house. My parents wanted to go back to Korea as soon as possible, but my sister had not yet been found.

Three months passed. My father said, "She must have died," and we all cried. We left for Korea on December 3 on a black-market cargo ship, leaving Masako behind with my pregnant sister.

For the first time in my life I was in my mother country, but I was bewildered, unable to speak Korean and ignorant of

Korean customs. My parents, who had once felt at ease, now seemed humiliated, receiving cold looks because they had returned from Japan. Derogatory words like *"Oay nom"* were thrown at them. Their fault was that they had once preferred Japan and now returned in miserable health, burdening their relatives, asking for food or land, and, due to the A-bomb, looking like monsters. We cried a lot because of emotional pain.

Finally the head of my father's side of the family gave him a share of a house and some land so that we would be able to start farming. Before long, I was admitted to a Korean Red Cross branch to learn the Korean language and to work as a nurse. I was assigned to provide injections preventing cholera, driving a jeep to rural areas.

Around that time, I met with several people in the mountains who had been A-bomb victims in Hiroshima. But I was hesitant to give them hope by telling them that I was in Hiroshima, too. I was hesitant because I could not take responsibility for them. My silence brought a bitter sense of guilt. Those people, without exception, stayed inside sheds, out of sight, putting potato juice on their wounds. American soldiers who came with me and saw the sheds asked why there were so many pigpens and concluded that the scarred Koreans were lepers. If I had known at that time that the A-bomb disease was such an awful thing, I would have told the American soldiers the truth. Those Koreans must have died there in the mountains since their conditions never improved.

I got married in 1947. My first baby died right after his birth. I had a second child, and my physical condition has declined since that time. Doctors could not diagnose my condition. Day by day my pain worsened. Complaints from my husband and his parents increased, with words like "Why don't you visit your parents?" or "Didn't you have this disease before you got married?" In the end, my son and I were forced back to my parents' house.

I got a job as a nurse at the navy hospital in Sa Chon, but my health would not allow me to keep working.

In 1958 I married a man who understood my situation. We went to Pusan and began our life together, and we had a daughter, then a son. But again my condition declined, and a year later I had an operation to remove a tumor near my ovary. I worried a lot about it, and I regretted remarrying. Symptoms of severe dizziness and a flushed face were occurring more often; the pain in my leg was increasing. Finally, I separated from my second husband.

After the normalization of Japanese-South Korean diplomatic relations in 1965, many books relating to the A-bomb came to Korea. I read one book with shock but didn't connect my condition to what I read. I then heard the term "A-bomb disease" for the first time from Japanese visitors, magazines, and radio broadcasts, which started coming to Korea around 1968. For the first time I wondered whether I had the A-bomb disease.

Later, I learned more about the fatal A-bomb disease directly from Japanese people and was convinced that I had it. I learned the term Burabura disease for the first time and realized that I had been affected by it. I failed in two marriages because of that disease and am still suffering from it, just waiting to die. My heart is wrung with grief when I think that I would not have become this ill if I had known about the A-bomb disease earlier.

The evil of the A-bomb disease must have attacked my children, too. My son from the first marriage began to suffer from severe anemia after coming back from the army. He had to be hospitalized for a long time because of a liver infection and serious jaundice. My daughter, too, has severe anemia.

They are the second generation of the A-bomb disease, children born to women who had been in Hiroshima at the time of the A-bomb. Who should take responsibility for them? I demand that the Japanese government open its eyes and ears to see and listen to the mothers and children who were victims of the A-bomb in Japan.

Many Koreans who were victims of the A-bomb are returning to Korea and still don't know that they have the disease. I am now a volunteer at the A-Bomb Victims Association. We visit the homes of patients, many of whom have deteriorated since our first visit. Sometimes we find that our patients have died. On these occasions we cry, "We wish they had taken us with them."

One day, at a meeting of the association, the anger piled up inside us for so long exploded: "We are going to die anyway. We should sell our few belongings, buy a small cargo ship, and go to Japan to demand a definite answer from the Japanese government. If we are detained, let's ask to be taken to Hiroshima and commit group suicide in the famous Peace Memorial Park."

Even though my mother, brother, and children have suffered so much due to the A-bomb, my wish is to die without hatred toward the Japanese people, who, as are we, are humans. To make that possible, I demand the Japanese government appropriately compensate Korean victims of the A-bomb.

If the Japanese took life seriously, wouldn't my wish come true?

Oay nom—Japanese dog
Burabura disease—"loitering" disease

Notes

Japan forcibly annexed Korea in 1910 in an attempt to expand its sphere of influence and control. In this process, the Japanese government forced many Korean families to relinquish their traditional patrimonial farmlands. Additionally, Japan expropriated the crops from much of the farmland they did not take over. This was done under the Japanese government's "land survey" and "plan to increase rice production" programs.

After the 1931 Manchurian Incident, Japan's 1899 Imperial Ordinance to Restrict Korean Entrance to Japan was abolished, and Koreans were urged to come to Japan to augment the labor force as Japan began to occupy China. In 1938 the Japanese government promulgated a national mobilization law in Korea that allowed it to bring Korean people to Japan by force for work in coal mines and munition factories. Additionally, many Koreans came to Japan during this period due to the extreme poverty of their homeland, brought on by the Japanese annexation and plundering of their resources. The total number of Koreans forced to come to Japan from 1939 to 1945 totaled about one million. In addition to this number, 4.5 million people were mobilized for forced labor inside Korea.

The Japanese government faced intense resistance from the Korean people, as they had in the 1919 Independence Movement. Because of this resistance, Japan adopted a strategy of disguising its oppression through a more cultural approach: Koreans were proclaimed "the Emperor's children" or "subjects of the Empire," just as the Japanese people were. This tactic led to a forced assimilation policy in which Koreans, even in Korea, were prohibited from speaking or writing their native language and were forced to adopt Japanese names.

Additionally, many young Korean women were taken to China, the Philippines, the Pacific Islands, or the Southern Front, where Japanese armies were stationed, and forced to become sexual slaves for the Japanese soldiers. An estimated 80,000 Korean women were put into this forced service, euphemistically called "comfort women" by the Japanese government and press, even to this day. According to the testimony of surviving women and those army officers now willing to talk about it, the women were collected by promises of good jobs in Japan. They were systematically hunted down by the Japanese army in Korea and taken from their homes and places of work by force.

tanka

Shoda Shinoe

Having made my way
through the fire,
I wait for dawn and
ride the corpses
floating down the river.

"Eat this when you come home!"
The child ran off
never to return.
Red is the tomato
offered at the house shrine.

tanka

Shoda Shinoe

In madness
a woman cries
"I left my child in the flames.
Now all I have
is my own life."

That person burned black,
wearing not even underwear,
must be a woman.
She passes, crying in madness,
breasts hanging down.

Let Us Not Forget Hiroshima / Auschwitz

Kurihara Sadako

What Auschwitz left behind is
striped prisoners' clothes
piles of children's shoes
heaps of little girls' ribbons
tableware that served both as bowls and chamber pots
soap made of human grease
fabrics woven of human hair

What Auschwitz left behind is
sorrow and anger impossible to end with their writings
even though the blue sky and seas of the world
are turned into ink
and the voices of the moaning are burned and killed in
gas chambers

What Hiroshima and Nagasaki left behind are
shadows printed on stones
black rain drawing lines on walls
radioactivity inside our bodies
children with microcephaly who were in their mothers'
    wombs at the time of the A-bomb
voices heard from the sky
voices heard from the bottom of the earth

Let us not forget Hiroshima/Auschwitz
let us not forget Nagasaki/Auschwitz

The first time was a mistake
the second time a betrayal
let us not forget our oath to the dead

Miyamaodamaki: *Fan Columbine*
from "Hiroshima: The Tales of Flowers" (1990)

Seki Chieko

Early summer, each year, I am reminded of the *miyamaodamaki* flower, its elegant figure stretching slightly downward. Its image is superimposed on the image of Mrs. Nagahashi Yaeko, my piano teacher who died in the A-bombing.

In May 1944, my sister and I started taking piano lessons under Mrs. Nagahashi after our relocation from Tokyo to Hiroshima. Mother, who always wanted the best of everything, found us "the finest music teacher in Hiroshima." She must have thought it would also be convenient since Mrs. Nagahashi taught at Hiroshima Women's Professional School, which occupied the same campus as our school.

Mrs. Nagahashi came from a family of famous musicians in Hiroshima. Her late husband as well as her brothers were musicians. Her only son, who had been in musical training, was at the war front.

My first impression of Mrs. Nagahashi was of an impeccably elegant elderly lady. I probably assumed her to be older than she actually was, as children usually do, although looking back, I think she might have been the same age that I am now, or slightly younger. Her image, however, was definitely *elderly lady* and never *old grandma*. I remember I was overwhelmed when I heard her serene voice for the first time. It gave me a sense of real music.

Mrs. Nagahashi had a nice, modern house located in Komachi, not far from the city's center. Its stylishness was rare in the Hiroshima of that time, and was hardly seen even in Tokyo. After entering the front door there was a small hall, where her students waited on a couch in the corner. The moment of my turn to enter the piano room made my heart jump because it was such a nice room. It was very spacious. At one end, two grand pianos were placed back to back. Several built-in cabinets reached the ceiling here and there along the wall. They were tightly packed with records, which made me wonder how long it would take to listen to all of them. Stained-glass panels were installed along the wall, giving the room a beautiful atmosphere.

Furthermore, the ceiling of this Western-style room was open to the second floor with a mezzanine. I could look up into the second floor above the sofas and chairs placed opposite the pianos. I thought the banister was charming. I had never before seen a private house with a Western-style room with such a railing, and her music room made me feel incomparably content.

Mrs. Nagahashi was very strict, as well as quiet and elegant. She did not compromise. When I made the slightest mistake, she said, "Practice one more time," and would not let me proceed to the next piece. Sometimes she told me sharply, "If you don't practice more, you will not play well."

Honestly speaking, I have no talent for piano. I could barely play easy sonatas after seven intermittent years of lessons. I did not like to practice. However, I had an excuse at that time. How could I practice with the war and people threatening me? When I played the piano sometimes they shouted, "Traitor! Stop playing the piano!" because many people frowned upon such things as music during wartime. I could not help feeling hesitant about practicing, and at that time pianos did not have dampers and their volume could not be controlled.

It was strange, though, that I never wanted to quit or skip my lessons in spite of the war, the lack of freedom to practice, or my extremely strict teacher. I think it was because something attracted me to Mrs. Nagahashi.

Around that time, students always had to carry air-raid hoods, and I, too, would go to school with one in a bag hanging from my shoulder. My mother had made the bag from a fabric normally used to pad kimono sashes. She must have thought the white color boring and embroidered some flowers on it. Gay things were a luxury. Luxury was the enemy. Even a little embroidery was frowned upon. I would half hide the flowers when I carried the bag, at the same time being thankful to her for making it.

One day Mrs. Nagahashi saw my bag and gave me a bright smile. "How beautiful it is! Did your mother make it?" she said, looking at it intently and holding it in her hand. She loved beautiful things. I felt very happy.

In 1945 the war situation became much more severe. It was cold, I recall, when Mrs. Nagahashi received the announcement of the death of her only son, who had a promising musical future as her successor. My teacher's lament was deep and pitiful. But she never skipped the lessons, and they were as strict as usual. Sometimes I could not stand my own laziness when she said calmly but resolutely, "You'd better practice one more time."

In May we were mobilized to clean up the remains of evacuated buildings in Zakoba town. This was the first work for us and lasted for three weeks, without Sundays off. My teacher's house was very near there. After work I went straight to her house and took my lesson.

It was on the last Sunday during this time that I saw someone selling flowers along the street and stopped as I hurried to my teacher's house. "Someone is selling something!" By that time, it had become very difficult to find anything to buy, even though the stores were open.

It was surprising enough just to see something being sold, and, when I went to look, I found a very beautiful flowering plant. On the short stem, which was ten or fifteen centimeters high, a purple flower with five petals was blooming, facing slightly downward. I looked at it for a long while.

"What is the name of this flower?"

"It's called *miyamaodamaki*. It is a perennial, so it will bloom every year in your garden."

Without hesitation I bought it with all of my allowance. I took it with me to my teacher's house, holding it very carefully. She cried out, "Oh! A flower! What is it called?"

"It's called *miyamaodamaki*."

"*Miyamaodamaki*," she repeated several times and gazed fixedly at it. "What an elegant flower!"

When I got home, I was asked by my mother, "What is the name of this flower?"

"*Miyamaodamaki*."

"*Miyamaodamaki*? With such a name, *miyama*, isn't this an alpine plant? I wonder if we are allowed to keep such a flower." She tilted her head, then in the end, decided to plant it under the pine tree by a small mound in our garden. Miyamaodamaki took root very well and kept blooming as the summer approached.

August came. We were scheduled to do cleanup work at another evacuation site. The location was again in Zakoba town, but closer to the city hall than the site in May.

The first day of work was August 5. It was a Sunday. I headed straight to my teacher's house. I played unusually well that day. She praised me and allowed me to proceed to the next song. I think it might have been the first lesson during which I was not scolded even once and only praised. I was so happy that I went home skipping with joy.

The next day the A-bomb was dropped. I happened to stay home that day because of diarrhea and miraculously escaped death. All of my classmates died instantly in Zakoba town. Mrs. Nagahashi was also one of the doomed.

I remember it was the beginning of October when my sister and I went to the central area for the first time after the bombing. We entered the ruins of our work site in Zakoba town, but I could not recognize anything. The whole area was burned and scorched. It was difficult to get even a suggestion of the old area, where I had worked at a rather large house with a mound and a big tree. Even the configuration of the area seemed to have changed. Burned lunch boxes, pieces of clothing, and baglike pieces of printed fabric were scattered on the ground, but there was no clue to clearly determine the site where my class had worked.

We walked through the burned ruins of Hiroshima's first middle school and continued north. We could see the city library to our left. It was burned and crumbled, but since it was a ferroconcrete building, the outside frame remained. Its basement had been turned into a storage area to collect corpses for burning.

Mrs. Nagahashi's house must have been in the rear of the alley. After looking around for awhile, we saw strange objects and stopped. Several pitch-black figures, like small drum cans, were lying on the ground. Immediately we gasped, realizing they were the records that had been tightly packed up to Mrs. Nagahashi's ceiling, now burned and fused together. It was a terrible scene. White bones still remained in the burned ruins. But those remains of the records looked even scarier to us than the bones.

To me, Mrs. Nagahashi's house was culture itself. It represented refinement that was seldom seen in Hiroshima at that brutal time. One bomb, instantly and thoroughly, destroyed it all.

Seeing us, someone who had been in the next yard approached. We heard from that person that Mrs. Nagahashi's death had been confirmed after her body had been discovered in the ruins of her house. Her body had looked like a praying figure. She might have been praying in front of the house altar for the repose of the souls of her husband and son at the time of her death.

In the fall of that year, the citizens in Hiroshima were filled with anxiety. There was a rumor that humans would not be able to live in Hiroshima for the next seventy years.

One late fall day, my mother, who had been in the backyard, suddenly cried out, "Oh my! Everyone, everyone come, look, look! Quick!" She was pointing in excitement to a small fig tree in the backyard with a new sprout shooting from its trunk. It was small, but it looked like a symbol of life. "It's all right, humans can live." My mother's voice was trembling.

The fig tree had been given to me by my sister as a present for my graduation from elementary school in March of the previous year. When we had to move to Hiroshima a month later, we could not bear to leave it behind and dug up the young tree, brought it to Hiroshima, and replanted it.

The following spring, every branch sprouted. The *miyamaodamaki* also bloomed beautifully. Looking at the purple flowers, lying quietly, always reminded me of Mrs. Nagahashi.

Miyamaodamaki kept blooming for a long time after that, and I don't remember when it disappeared from our garden. Many years later I came home after six-and-a-half years in America, and six months after that, in 1976, my mother died from cancer. I rushed to my mother's house from Yokohama. A day after the funeral I went out to the garden, finding myself unexpectedly remembering the flower. I saw no trace of it at all.

Was that flower really *miyamaodamaki*, I used to wonder? I decided it was time to check it out and went to a library to look it up in an illustrated dictionary. "*Miyamaodamaki*, an alpine plant of odamaki family. It blooms with five purple petals in early summer." It was as I had thought. But the next line perplexed me. "It is native to the high mountains from the north of middle Japan to Hokkaido." Was it possible to bring what was native to the north of middle Japan to Hiroshima and watch it take root there and bloom?

Furthermore, I found that there was a *yamaodamaki* in the same family that grew in the gardens of family homes. The dictionary said that it grew commonly in Kyushu or western Japan. This must be what it was, but it is also said to have a yellow center. I was sure my *miyamaodamaki* had been all purple.

The dictionary had color pictures of both kinds. The yellow center of *yamaodamaki* was too striking and rather gaudy. The elegance of my *miyamaodamaki* perfectly fit the picture of the *miyamaodamaki* in the dictionary. There is no way to confirm it now, for my *miyamaodamaki* is forever gone.

Komachi — a district of Hiroshima
Zakoba — a district of Hiroshima

haiku

Kakinami Sonoko

red dragonflies
your normal sky
a nuclear sky

A-bomb anniversary
I open my five fingers
against the sunset

A-bomb anniversary
eyeless young fish
wander the hills

The Entrance to the Future

Kurihara Sadako

Here is the entrance to the future,
a human graveyard.
Its roof draws a streamlined arc
three feet above the earth.
Before it
is the museum of First Tragedy.
Through its entrance
a mercurylike light shines white from the fountain.
When nobody is near, the dead
may slip out of their stone caskets
to go sip trickling water
for still-burning throats.

Here is the entrance to the future.
From all over the world
people come for casual visits, a camera hanging on each chest.
The truth is
they come to witness their own destiny.
Inside
lovers turn pale, standing without motion
before metal or glass tableware
with melted human bones stuck together like candies.
Mothers hold children, embracing them,
for fear of their being killed.

Here is the entrance to the future.
Can the world go through this,
bring carbonized ruins of humans back to life?

Lost in the dim-lighted exhibition hall,
a dove perching on a windowsill
tilts its head.

Selected Author Biographies

*The authors' names are given in the Japanese order
of family name first, given name second.*

Fukuda Sumako

Born in 1919, Sumako is a survivor of the A-bomb in Nagasaki.
Her poem "Talking to Myself," published in a major newspaper, made the nation aware of the hard lives and emotional
suffering of A-bomb survivors. Right after the nuclear attack in
1945 she became actively involved in antinuclear movements.
In 1969 she received the Tamura Toshiko Prize, a Japanese literary prize for women, for her documentary essay describing the
lives of survivors of nuclear attacks. She died in 1971 at the age
of fifty-two.

Ishikawa Itsuko

Born in 1933, Itsuko graduated from Ochanomizu University.
In 1976 she started yearly field trips to Hiroshima for the students of the middle school where she was a teacher. Since 1982
Itsuko has been publishing the newsletter *Thinking of
Hiroshima and Nagasaki*. She is one of the prominent writers
who document concerns of A-bomb survivors and other mi-
nority groups in Japan. She received an Earth Award in 1986
for her poetry collection *Chidorigafuchi ni Ikimashitaka* (Have
You Been to Chidorigafuchi?).

Her publications (in Japanese) include: *Wolf Us*, poetry, Mr.
H. Award recipient, 1960; *Children and War*, poetry, 1976;
Continuing Prayers, poetry, 1982; *Swimming Horse*, poetry, 1984;
Teacher's Depression, essays, 1987; *Voices of the Dead*, essays, 1990.

Kurihara Sadako

Born in 1913 in Hiroshima, Sadako started writing poems and
tanka at the age of thirteen. She graduated from Kobe
Women's High School. A Hiroshima A-bomb survivor, she

founded Chugoku Bunka Renmei Culture Association and published the first issue of *Chugoku Bunka*. Since then she has been deeply involved in the antinuclear movement through her literary activities. In 1969 Sadako founded a citizens' group, "Gensuikin Hiroshima Haha no Kai" (Hiroshima Mothers' Group against A-Bombs and H-Bombs), and published an anthology of poetry about Hiroshima, *The River of Flame Running in Japan*, which she distributed at the Sixth World Conference against A-Bombs and H-Bombs. The following year she started the journal, *The Rivers in Hiroshima*, that continued through five bimonthly issues. In 1962 Sadako organized a publishing committee and privately published *The Songs of Hiroshima* with parallel versions in English and Japanese.

For almost fifty years now Sadako has tried to make people aware of the danger of nuclear warfare, not only for the peoples in the Pacific Islands and the Pacific Rim, whose suffering has gone unnoticed by the world because of their isolation, but for humanity as a whole, since she feels there can be no lasting peace as long as we live under the threat of nuclear attacks. To achieve this, in addition to her publications listed below, she edited journals *(Testimony of Hiroshima and Nagasaki*, 1982), wrote essays *(Embracing the Core Scene of Hiroshima*, published by Shishu Kanko no Kai in 1975), and attended numerous conferences, among them the NGO International Symposium in 1977 on "The Reality of the A-Bomb"; the 1980 Pacific Block International Conference Against Nuclear Development in Honolulu, Hawaii; the 1982 International Literature Conference in Köln, Germany; the 1982 International Conference of Educators for Disarmament; and was involved in the 1983 Conference of Asian Writers in Hiroshima, protesting against nuclear development, poverty, and oppression.

Her publications include: *The Black Egg*, 1946; *The River of Flame Running in Japan*, 1960; *The Songs of Hiroshima*, 1962; *I, A Hiroshima Witness*, 1967; *Documents about Hiroshima Twenty-Four Years Later*, 1970 (Shincho sha); *Hiroshima: The Future*

Scene, 1974 (Shishu Kanko no Kai); *When I Say Hiroshima,* 1976 (Sanitsu Shobo); *Nuclear Emperor and the Victims of the A-Bomb,* essays, 1978 (Sanitsu Shobo); *The Future Begins Here,* 1979 (Shishu Kanko no Kai); *Fairy Tales of the Nuclear Age,* 1982 (Shishu Kanko no Kai); *Living in the Nuclear Age,* essays, 1982 (Sanitsu Shobo); A personal report in *1945, An International Anthology,* 1984 (Kiepenhauer, West Germany); *Genbaku Kashu, Kushu,* an anthology of tanka and haiku about the A-bomb, editor, 1991; *Genbaku shishu,* an anthology of poems about the A-bomb, editor, 1991; *Hiroshima in Question,* essays, 1992 (Sanichi Shobo).

Maruki Toshi
Born in 1912, Toshi graduated from Women's Art School. She came to Hiroshima right after the A-bomb was dropped. In 1950 she started to create artworks called *Pictures of the A-Bomb.* Toshi received the International Peace Prize in 1952. *Hiroshima no Pika,* originally a children's picture book, was given the Mildred L. Bachelder Award in 1980. She is the recipient of other international prizes for her artistic achievements.

Seki Chieko
Born in 1932 in Osaka, Chieko is a graduate of Waseda University, where she majored in Russian literature. Currently she is editing director of *National Women's Newspaper,* after having been a journalist for the *Mainichi* newspaper. She was the recipient of the thirty-third Japan Essayist Club Award for her book *My Classmates Who Died from the A-Bomb.*

Shoda Shinoe
Like Sadako and Sumako, Shinoe is a survivor of the A-bomb, a fact that had a decisive impact on her professional and private life. During the years following the nuclear attack there was a law prohibiting the publication of anything related to the A-bomb. Shinoe ignored the law and in 1947 privately published *Sange,* a collection of her tanka. Unfortunately she did

not live long enough to see the publication of her second tanka collection, *Sarusuberi,* published in 1966. All her life she had been suffering from A-Bomb Disease, which eventually caused her death from breast cancer in 1965.

Yamaguchi Misao
Born 1955 in Hiroshima City, Misao was raised in Hiroshima and works there at a school for disabled children.

Yamaoka Michiko
Born in 1930 in Hiroshima, Michiko spent her high-school years in halberd and bamboo spear practice as well as in labor service. In 1945 she was mobilized into work at a telephone office, where she was a victim of the atomic bombing. Her mother also suffered injuries and together with Michiko was moved from shelter to shelter until they were finally settled in 1947.

In 1949 Michiko met with other women bombing victims under the auspices of a local Christian church. Out of that and future meetings she was chosen to travel to the United States for medical treatment. She then returned to Japan and began work at a dressmaking school.

Her father had died when Michiko was three and her mother died in 1979. Following her mother's death Michiko was hospitalized for six months. The death of her mother precipitated a major change in Michiko's life and she became an ardent storyteller, relating her experience of the A-bombing.

From 1980 to 1983 Michiko worked at a nursery school. She is currently vice director at the World Friendship Center.

Lequita Vance-Watkins lives in Carmel, California, where she is the executive director of the San Jose Center for Poetry and Literature. She received a California Arts Council Artists Fellowship for Literature in 1993, and her haiku and tanka have won numerous awards. Vance-Watkins's poems, articles, translations, and interviews have been widely anthologized and have appeared in such places as *The San Francisco Review of Books, Amelia, Loon Feather,* and *Poetry Flash.* An active promoter of poetry and organizer of frequent readings and workshops, she is also a professional interior designer.

Aratani Mariko was born in Japan. She graduated from the Tokyo University of Fine Art and Music (*Tokyo Gaigutsu Daigaku*) and has been a professional musician and translator in both the United States and Japan. She and cotranslator Jane Hirshfield won the 1987 Columbia University Translation Award for *The Ink Dark Moon: Love Poems by Ono no Kamachi and Izumu Shikibu, Women of the Ancient Court of Japan* (Charles Scribner's Sons, 1988). Aratani has published many Japanese translations of English works. She lives with her husband, daughter, and two black cats in Ann Arbor, Michigan, where she is an instructor and interpreter of Japanese.

Designed by Will Powers
Typeset in Galliard and Tiepolo typefaces
by Stanton Publication Services
Printed on acid-free 55-pound Quebecor Liberty paper
by Quebecor-Fairfield

More translations from Milkweed Editions

Amen
Poems by Yehuda Amichai
Translated from the Hebrew
by the author and Ted Hughes

The Art of Writing
Lu Chi's Wen Fu
Translated from the Chinese
by Sam Hamill

Astonishing World
Selected Poems of Ángel González
Translated from the Spanish
by Steven Ford Brown

Circe's Mountain
Stories by Marie Luise Kaschnitz
Translated from the German
by Lisel Mueller

Clay and Star
Contemporary Bulgarian Poets
Translated and edited
by Lisa Sapinkopf and Georgi Belev

The House in the Sand
Prose Poems by Pablo Neruda
Translated from the Spanish
by Dennis Maloney and Clark Zlotchew

Mouth to Mouth
Poems by Twelve Contemporary Mexican Women
Edited by Forrest Gander

Trusting Your Life to Water and Eternity
Twenty Poems by Olav H. Hauge
Translated from the Norwegian
by Robert Bly